IMAGES
of America

FORSYTH
COUNTY
AN ALBUM FROM THE
GARLAND BAGLEY COLLECTION

GARLAND C. BAGLEY (1909–1984). The images in this volume are those collected by Garland Bagley for his intended use in the publication of a history of Forsyth County, Georgia. His untimely death in 1984 preceded the publication of his work. However, two volumes were published posthumously—in 1985 and 1990, respectively. In 1995, Marie Bagley Roper donated her brother's papers, photographs, books, and documents to the Historical Society of Forsyth County, Inc. The materials amassed by historian Garland Bagley are now referred to as the Garland Bagley Collection.

IMAGES
of America

FORSYTH COUNTY
AN ALBUM FROM THE
GARLAND BAGLEY COLLECTION

Annette Bramblett
Historical Society of Forsyth County, Inc.

ARCADIA

First published 1998
Copyright © Annette Bramblett
Historical Society of Forsyth County, Inc., 1998

ISBN 0-7524-0419-9

Published by Arcadia Publishing,
an imprint of the Chalford Publishing Corporation,
One Washington Center, Dover, New Hampshire 03820.
Printed in Great Britain

Library of Congress Cataloging-in-Publication Data applied for

Contents

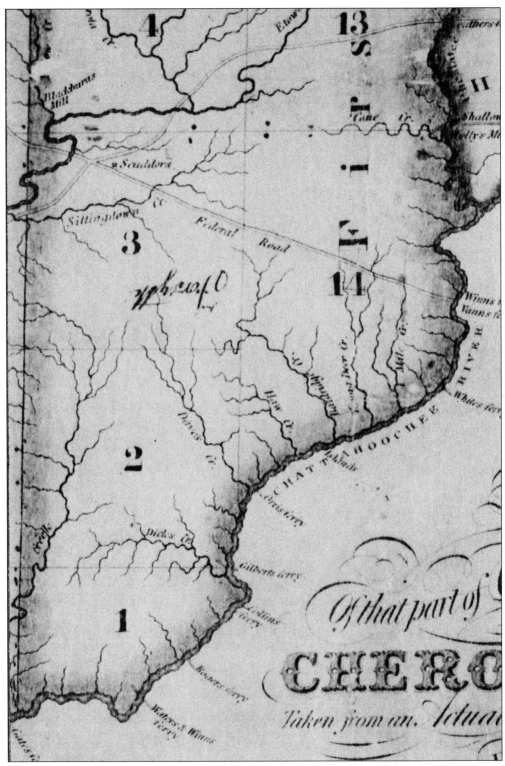

This is the earliest existing map of the Forsyth County area, drawn by John Bethune in 1831.

Introduction

Prior to 1832, the northwest corner of Georgia as far east as present-day Forsyth County was Cherokee Indian Territory. The State Legislature, desiring to open this area to white settlers, enacted legislation which created the original Cherokee County in 1831. Although the act provided for the peaceful intermingling of whites and Native Americans—with the Cherokees being permitted to retain ownership of their individual improvements—the spirit of the law was not fulfilled.

Gold having been discovered in 1828 near Auraria in the region now known as Lumpkin County, the whites were clamoring for land. The former Cherokee Territory was surveyed in 1832 and awarded to fortunate drawers in a lottery system at Milledgeville. The land which would become Forsyth County was plotted into 60-acre "gold lots" in the 1st, 2nd, 3rd, and 14th districts. As expected, gold was found in the county's streams, for Forsyth lies in both the Dahlonega and Hall County Gold Belts.

Created from the original Cherokee County by an Act of December 3, 1832, Forsyth County was named in honor of Governor John Forsyth. A graduate of Princeton, Forsyth had served as a Georgia lawyer, attorney general, congressman, senator, governor, minister to Spain, and secretary of state under Presidents Jackson and Van Buren.

The historical marker, placed by the Georgia Historical Commission on the courthouse lawn in Cumming, the seat of Forsyth County, proclaims the first officers of the county as of April 20, 1833: John Blaylock, clerk of superior court; Thomas Burford, county surveyor; and Alston B. Welborn, coroner. On January 31, 1834, Hubbard Barker was commissioned sheriff.

Subsequent to the establishment of the county, a building was needed in which to transact the affairs of government. First the home of William Hammond was used, followed by the construction of a log courthouse. Then in 1839, a large frame house was erected in the center of the public square. This structure housed government offices until the first brick courthouse was built in 1854. After several decades, the brick courthouse fell into disrepair and was replaced by a second brick edifice, which graced the square from 1905 until it was destroyed by fire on November 5, 1973.

While settlers were clearing land and erecting cabins, merchants establishing their businesses, and elected officials pursuing government business, the Cherokees were seeking to adapt to the ways of the white man. After the invention of the Cherokee syllabary by Sequoyah, the Cherokees had encouraged their people to become literate and had even set up a print shop at the Cherokee capitol of New Echota for producing their own newspaper, the *Cherokee Phoenix*. Their justice system was likewise patterned after that of the white settlers.

By 1838, the whites, desirous of taking over Cherokee holdings, launched an effort to expel Native Americans from their homeland. Valuations on Cherokee improvements established the basis for payments to them as those who had not intermarried with the whites or who did not possess valued skills in their communities were herded west on the infamous Trail of Tears.

Vestiges of Forsyth County's Cherokee heritage, however, remain to this day. The Old Federal Road, built in the 1800s, traversed two of Chief James Vann's holdings. Vann's tavern near his ferry on the Chattahoochee River became the Monte Boyd home before it was moved to New Echota near Calhoun and restored in 1958 to save it from the rising waters of Lake Sidney Lanier. Another lodge owned by Vann, also called Blackburn's Inn and Buffington's Tavern, was purportedly the inn where President Monroe, traveling incognito, spent a night or two in 1819. This tavern remains near its original site above the Etowah River in northwest Forsyth County.

The Cherokees having departed for western lands, the settlers were free to mine the available gold to the extent their energies and finances could afford. Yet over the years Forsyth County became an agrarian area and remained so until after the mid twentieth century. Indeed farmhouses, barns, and other "outbuildings" dotted the landscape, with mills and general stores interspersed as needed.

A change occurred in the late 1930s, however, in the system of agriculture. Since the Great Depression had left the area virtually destitute, with cotton prices dropping to an all-time low on world markets, the one-crop practice, of necessity, came to an end. The alternative "crop" with which farmers began to experiment was chickens. The poultry industry became a rapid success and brought prosperity to the locale previously plagued with poverty. And to heighten the economic boost, Wilson and Company established a processing plant in Cumming in 1943 and took on a sizable workforce.

Although Forsyth County is experiencing a different kind of prosperity today—a land boom with burgeoning population—many of the old landmarks remain. Sawnee Mountain, which bears the name of a lesser Cherokee chief, rises 1,967 feet and is visible from virtually all of the county's boundaries. From atop the mountain, one has only to look east for a magnificent view of Lake Sidney Lanier, flooded in 1957 by the U.S. Army Corps of Engineers. An occasional farmhouse also serves as a reminder of a vanishing way of life.

But it wasn't landmarks that created the history of the region. It was people—from distinguished leaders and rugged pioneers to professionals and dirt farmers. From Col. Hiram Parks Bell, lawyer, congressman, and Confederate colonel, to Hardy Strickland, who served in the Confederate Congress, Forsyth County's leaders served her well. On the homefront, pastors helped strengthen the moral fiber of the community, while doctors, such as Ansel Strickland, the Mashburns, Brambletts, Lipscombs, and others, cared for the county's physical needs. Moreover, businessmen, including the Heards and Otwells, offered essential goods and services. It was the common man, though, who, by his resourceful nature and practical experience, met the challenge in difficult times and persevered from humble beginnings to a better way of life.

This book is intended to showcase the people, places, and events which have contributed to the development of Forsyth County and which have rendered its history unique.

One

Early Days

The Vann Tavern at Frogtown testifies to Forsyth County's Cherokee heritage. It was the scene of the killing of Chief James Vann in 1809 and overnight stay of President Monroe in 1819. Although in a sad state of disrepair, the building is still standing. The lodge has also been known as Blackburn's Inn and Buffington's Tavern for two of its operators.

The farm buildings surrounding the Vann Tavern are a part of the estate of the late Ernest Sherrill. The tavern has been moved across the road from its original site where the Sherrill house now stands and tends to blend in with the other structures in a cow pasture, where it usually remains unnoticed.

Native American influence is seen in this photo of the first bridge over the Etowah River and the site of Blackburn's fish trap, for which the government allowed Blackburn $50 during the Cherokee Removal of 1838. Nearby is the mouth of Red Bank Creek, now called Bannister Creek. The bridge currently in use is around the bend from this site.

The cemetery is named for Lewis Blackburn, one of the operators of Vann's Tavern. After Vann was called out of the tavern and fatally shot in 1809, it is believed that he was buried in this cemetery, but his gravesite, once marked, is now unidentifiable. A number of mixed breeds and black slaves are also buried here. The cemetery is located approximately 1/4 mile from the tavern.

Siding on the Monte Boyd home near the banks of the Chattahoochee River masked its true identity. It was originally built as a tavern by Chief James Vann near his ferry on the river. When Lake Lanier was flooded in the late 1950s, the structure was moved to New Echota near Calhoun, Georgia, and the siding was removed to restore the tavern to its appearance in the early 1800s.

Visitors to New Echota, the capitol of the Cherokee Nation, may view Chief Vann's tavern today because it has been restored and imagine it in its original setting beside the Old Federal Road near the Chattahoochee River in Forsyth County just across the line from Hall County. That same individual may picture, too, the weary traveler sleeping in an unheated room with

only a blanket for warmth after an evening of perhaps drinking, card playing, and rough companionship. And the following morning, unbeknownst to the guest at the inn, his horse might have been replaced by an inferior animal to allow him to be run down, robbed, and killed. Chief Vann was not always a charming host.

This petroglyph, once located near Mount Tabor Baptist Church in the northwest section of the county, is believed to have been carved by members of the Red Bank Tribe. It was first noted by George White in his *Historical Collections of Georgia*, copyright 1855. Approximately a century later, it was found by author Margaret Perryman and described in an article in the magazine *Early Georgia*.

William Rogers (1805–1870) resided along the Chattahoochee River in the area which would later be incorporated into Fulton County. Part Cherokee, he was the son of John Rogers and Sarah Cordery. William Rogers was a member of the Treaty Party when the Treaty of New Echota in 1835 provided for the removal of the Cherokees living east of the Mississippi River.

The Key Hole House was situated across the Chattahoochee River from Forsyth County in the community known as Wooley's Ford. Members of the John Murrell Gang operated from this dwelling and created considerable anguish in the early days of Forsyth County. Within its walls, unspeakable acts were reportedly carried out and the darkest of secrets hidden from view.

So great were the crimes perpetrated by the Murrell Gang that a sizable reward was issued for the capture of its members. Carrying out its dastardly deeds about 1834 or 1835, the gang earned the reputation as "The Most Ruthless Gang of All Time." Its leader frequently posed as a preacher, while his cohorts robbed those gathered to hear his sermons. Many a horse disappeared from these religious gatherings.

15

The Pascoe House sits on gold-bearing land on the Forsyth-Cherokee border. It was built by John Pascoe for his bride in the late 1830s, but Pascoe died as a result of mercuric poisoning from his mining lab before the marriage could take place. The property passed to his brother, Samuel, and later became the superintendent's residence for the Franklin Gold Mines.

The interior of the Pascoe House was surprisingly ornate for its era. The living room walls were adorned with stately wainscoting, and the carved wooden mantel, pictured here, was imported from England. No doubt Pascoe's bride would have been duly impressed had she not received the sad news of her fiance's death and returned to her home in England.

Remains of the stamp mill from the early gold mining days can still be seen from the Etowah River bridge on Yellow Creek Road. At this mill, ore-laden rocks were crushed to free the gold contained therein. The ore was taken from the river and from a tunnel dug beneath the river. Thus, the mill's location on the banks of the Etowah was a matter of convenience.

The scenic Etowah River, dividing Forsyth and Cherokee Counties, was the site of successful gold-mining activities. Near the Pascoe and Franklin mines, an aerial view shows that the river forms the outline of an eagle. Forsyth County author Forest Wade even entitled his book on the Cherokees and their gold *Cry of the Eagle*. Downstream from the eagle, the river was dammed for a chlorination plant.

The Terry-Settle House is one of the oldest structures in Forsyth County and is currently undergoing major restoration efforts. Located on land lot #1079 in the Shakerag community, the house, built in the late 1830s, came into the Terry family in 1866, when John G. Terry married Elizabeth Cawley. After a series of owners, George Thomas Settle and his wife, Sarah Cottrell, purchased the land in 1892, and the house remained in the ownership of Terry and Settle descendents until recent years. Mr. Toy Settle and his sister, "Miss Ida," were the last members of the family to reside within its walls. When the Olde Atlanta Club purchased the property, the Historical Society of Forsyth County and later the Georgia Trust for Historic Preservation saved the structure from extinction. It is now being restored by new owners who plan to live in the historic dwelling.

Two
Changing Times

Churches, the core of community life, supported pioneer settlers through the hardships of daily living. Though church buildings changed from log cabins to frame buildings, then to the brick structures that are seen today, the religious beliefs on which they were founded remained constant. The church pictured here, Concord Baptist, served its congregation through several decades of this century. Concord was founded in the late 1830s.

The 1847 map of Forsyth County by William S. Bonner clearly defines the boundaries of the county, including the southernmost portion in District 1, which was removed to form Milton County, and later incorporated into Fulton County in the 1930s. The Old Federal Road ran from the Chattahoochee River through the northern part of the county and crossed the Etowah River at Frogtown, only a few miles from the Franklin Gold Mines. In the early days, the Chattahoochee River formed the eastern and southern boundaries. One should note that the county seat, Cumming, is identified as well as the communities of Hightower, Vickery Creek, and Big Creek. Near the northeastern boundary, the confluence of the Chestatee and Chattahoochee Rivers is currently a part of Lake Sidney Lanier and "River Forks" is the name given to a Corps of Engineers park near the site.

Forsyth County's first brick courthouse, which replaced a frame building on the site in the center of the Cumming Square, was erected in 1854 and served until another brick structure was built in 1905. This fine courthouse boasted no modern conveniences: it was heated by fireplaces in winter and the only water inside was that carried in from the well nearby.

Photographed in front of the first brick courthouse is Izzie Chamblee Otwell, wife of Chess Otwell, holding the horse. The ladies in the buggy are Lena Lipscomb Martin, Nannie Lipscomb Hays, and Daisy Lipscomb Hockenhull. From the youthful appearance of the young women, the photograph was likely taken before they were married and the subjects identified at a later date.

Postmarks shown are of local country post offices: Vickery Creek, Sevier, and Nettie. Others, abandoned in 1903 or 1904 when Rural Free Deliveries began, included Hightower, Warsaw, Coal Mountain, Allenville, Vickery, Marshalltown, Crossville, Mimsville, Hartford, Big Creek, Sheltonville, Ashland, Lewiston, Dave's Creek, Sawnee Mountain, Bethlehem, Cuba, Matt, Lane, Spot, Drew, Itley, Brown's Bridge, New Prospect, Pleasant Grove, Haw Creek, Wolfden, Oscarville, New Prospect, Ducktown, Southard, Heardsville, Ami, Pleasant, Settendown, Tatum, Silver City, Chestatee, Mortimer, Echols, Storeville, Piedmont, Gravel Springs, Odell, Solo, Novetta, Harmony, Liverpool, Omega, Mish, Otis, Fawcett, Velvie, Albert, Arch, and Frona. Postmasters on July 1, 1889, were Mrs. S.A. Hutchins, John W. Bailey, George F. Bagwell, J.P. Heard, I.S. Clements, Jas. E. Echols, George L. Heard, Jesse M. Sheffield, J.C. Blackstock, W.L. Chamblee, G.H. Collins, Jesse E. Eades, Samuel S. Sims, and C.E. Orr.

Augustus L. Glover in his mule-powered buggy demonstrates one form of travel in the early days. Transportation was confined to foot travel, wagons, buggies, or horseback, as Forsyth County had no railroad. Glover's mule would be expected to "wear many hats," for he would also pull the plow and assist his master in clearing the land.

Pictured is the town of Cumming looking north in 1910. Far from its primitive beginnings in the mid-1830s, the county seat had already evolved into a larger entity with businesses clustering near the courthouse square and homes and churches on the periphery. Cumming First Baptist Church may be noted in the upper left corner of this photograph.

As the town of Cumming grew over the years, transportation also experienced a monumental change. The automobile came on the scene and negotiated the muddy, unpaved roads of the county. (For many years U.S. Highway 19, paved in the early 1930s, was the only paved road in the county.) The first automobile in the county was later sold to Roy P. Otwell as Forsyth County's first pre-owned car.

"Cumming No. 2" was Dr. Ansel Strickand's 1910 International. The horseless carriage was a chain drive, two cylinder, with about 15 horsepower. It ran at top speeds of about 30–35 m.p.h. The engine was under the front seat. The magnificent machine was hand cranked from the side and featured solid rubber tires.

Roy Otwell's 1914 Model T captured attention on whichever street or lane Otwell chose to enter. These gentlemen of Cumming cut a fine figure as they posed before the new automobile. Pictured, from left to right, are Sport Merritt, Roy Otwell, Leland Pirkle, Roy Strickland, and Ed Merritt. Onlookers appear to appreciate the sight.

Augustus Woodliff enjoyed being chauffeured about town and elsewhere in his 1915 Model T Ford with Jeff Woodliff at the wheel. The Model T was a popular automobile and added its share to the hustle and bustle about town as it intermingled with horses, mules, wagons, pedestrians, and agricultural products for sale. Indeed, transportation had entered a more complex age.

This 1920 map of Forsyth County by the National Map Company indicates numerous changes from the map of 1847. The southernmost part of the county has been removed and added to Milton County. Communities are evidenced throughout the county. Forsyth's mountain and enduring landmark is incorrectly labeled. Sawnee Mountain is located a short distance northwest of Cumming.

By the twentieth century, bridges had begun to replace ferries. The earliest bridges were wooden, covered structures. Later iron spans, such as this bridge over the Etowah at Frogtown, were erected. The bridge in the photograph was destroyed and later replaced by its modern equivalent, a concrete one built to withstand the weight of car and truck traffic, which proliferates daily.

From the one-room schoolhouses of pioneer times, the educational buildings increased notably. The Mount Zion School at Oscarville in 1924 shows the architectural features of a structure erected to meet the needs of the community's youth. The number of students pictured seemed large for its day but was merely a forerunner of the burgeoning school-age population to come.

Forsyth Farm Homes Get Electricity

Rural electrification brought lifestyle changes and increased opportunities to the people in agrarian Forsyth County. When the switch was thrown on June 22, 1939, by members of the board of directors of the power company, current flowed through 168 miles of line and served more than 750 homes. Several thousand residents were on hand to celebrate the momentous event.

From the horse-and-buggy days to the era of the first automobiles, change occurred in modes of transportation. Pictured here is Forsyth County's first new airplane, a two-place Piper J-3. The date was 1946 and more air miles were to be logged in the near future. The Piper's landing area was any field with sufficient space for it to touch down safely.

By 1947, a new plane was on the scene. This aviation marvel was Forsyth County's first three-place aircraft, a Piper Cruiser. Like the Piper J-3, it, too, required merely a pasture or open field for take-offs and landings. In later years, Mathis Airport in southeast Forsyth would open to small aircraft seeking to fly in and out of the county.

Three
Portrait Gallery

Dr. Rader Hugh Bramblett, a second generation physician, was born on October 5, 1886, and died on December 16, 1952. He married Ida Palestine Garrett (born on April 18, 1883, and died September 29, 1959), daughter of Civil War soldier John Alvin Garrett, on December 18, 1904, and graduated from the Georgia College of Eclectic Medicine and Surgery in 1911. Bramblett was the son of Dr. Martin Truman Bramblett and was a fourth generation Forsyth Countian.

MAYORS OF CUMMING

ROY P. OTWELL, SR.

J. G. PUETT

FORD GRAVITT

A. B. TOLLISON

MARCUS MASHBURN, JR.

MARCUS MASHBURN, SR.

JOHN D. BLACK

GEORGE INGRAM

HENRY L. "SNACKS" PATTERSON

These portraits of Cumming mayors greet visitors as they enter City Hall. The gentlemen pictured and their terms of office include the following: Roy P. Otwell (1928–1956 and 1959–1960), J.G. Puett (1918–1919), Ford Gravitt (1970–present), A.B. Tollison (1926–1927), Dr. Marcus Mashburn Jr. (1957–1958), Dr. Marcus Mashburn Sr. (1917, 1961–1966), John D. Black (1922–1923), George Ingram (1966–1970), and Henry L. Patterson (1920–1921).

John Forsyth (1780–1841) was the governor for whom Forsyth County was named. A native of Frederick County, Virginia, he was a graduate of Princeton, a gifted Georgia lawyer, attorney general of Georgia, congressman, senator, minister to Spain, governor, and secretary of state under Presidents Jackson and Van Buren. Forsyth County was created by an Act of 1832 and named in his honor.

George Stewart Cunningham was born on February 3, 1849, and died June 1900. He is listed in the 1870 United States census as residing in the Coal Mountain District of Forsyth County. Cunningham married Milbry Mathis (1851–1938), the daughter of John Mathis (1809–1893, died in Forsyth County) and his wife, Malissa, who were married about 1831. George S. Cunningham and Milbry Mathis were married on November 21, 1869, in Forsyth County.

Col. Hiram Parks Bell (1827–1907) was a lawyer, statesman, author, and Confederate soldier. In 1861, he served as a delegate from Forsyth County to the Georgia Secession Convention; as state senator (1862); in the Second Confederate Congress (1863–1865); and as United States congressman (1872–1876 and 1877–1880). His most noted work is entitled *Men and Things*.

Dr. Homer V.M. Miller was Forsyth County's first medical doctor. After he practiced medicine in the early days of the county, he moved away and later became a U.S. senator from Georgia (but not from Forsyth County). Dr. Miller was also a powerful orator. He is buried at Myrtle Hill Cemetery in Rome, Georgia.

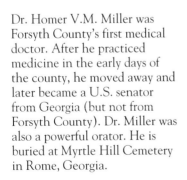

William Willis Vaughan, born 1805 in Virginia, was the son of James M. and Martha Susanah Vaughan. He married Anna Williams about 1825 and later migrated to Forsyth County, where he settled near Cumming. He became a real estate trader soon after the county was created and later became a Justice of the Peace about August 1, 1836. He also owned 6 acres of improved land and 96 acres of unimproved land.

Thomas Jefferson Pilgrim was born on July 24, 1817, and died on June 15, 1890. In 1855, he was instrumental, along with Samuel M. Reese and Ellison Hope, in funding the construction of Antioch Baptist Church. He served with the Kellogg Rifles in the Civil War and was elected captain in March 1862; then he was elected colonel of the First Georgia Militia in 1862.

Alexander Herring is pictured with his wife, the former Louisa Brown, whom he married on August 12, 1855, in Forsyth County. The Herring household is listed in the 1860 U.S. Census of Forsyth County, the only listing for this couple. Alexander Herring served with the "Forsyth County Cavalry" in the Georgia State Guards during the Civil War.

William Mathis (born July 5, 1846, and died November 14, 1944) was the eighth child of John and Malissa Mathis. At a very young age he served in the Civil War. In this photograph, he is posing with a borrowed gun, because he was deemed too young to carry a rifle. He married Sarah Bagley in Forsyth County on October 25, 1869. Both are buried in Piney Grove cemetery.

Abijah John Julian (born December 2, 1842, and died June 18, 1921) was the son of George Hampton Julian and Adeline Webster Julian. His wife, the former Minnie Bailey, the daughter of Dr. Samuel S. Bailey and Julia Ann Thompson Bailey, had a long and distinguished career as an educator. Abijah John Julian served in the Civil War in the Kellogg Rifles.

On the left is Lorena Groover, the daughter of W.J. Groover. Charlotte Strickland, on the right, was the daughter of Dr. Ansel Strickland and his first wife, Julia Hockenhull Strickland. Lorena became Mrs. Cliff Vaughan and Charlotte became Mrs. Mac Puett, the mother of Mrs. Juliette Puett Maxwell. Charlotte was raised by her father and step-mother, Mamie Rogers Strickland.

Born in 1858, Dr. Ansel Strickland was the son of Henry and Ann Elizabeth Smith Strickland. He married Julia Hockenhull, the daughter of Dr. John and Mary Hutchins Hockenhull, and later Mary Lavina Rogers, the daughter of Robert Nicholas Rogers. After an outstanding career as a physician and scientist, Dr. Strickland died in 1914 and was buried in Cumming Cemetery.

James Riley Bramblett, a pioneer settler in Forsyth County, was born in 1818, died in 1885, and was buried in Friendship Baptist Church's cemetery. He first married Margaret Roberts on February 7, 1841, and then Elizabeth Stewart on November 5, 1857, and later Cinderella Salter Bolin in 1860. The Bramblett doctors of Forsyth County are descendents of James Riley and Margaret Roberts Bramblett.

Dr. Martin Truman Bramblett, the son of James Riley Bramblett, was born in 1853 and died in 1911. He married Mary Indiana Hawkins, the daughter of Robert Hawkins, on April 1, 1874. Three of their sons became physicians: Dr. James C. Bramblett, Dr. Rader Hugh Bramblett, and Dr. Joel Thaddeus Bramblett. A grandson, Dr. Rupert H. Bramblett, son of Dr. Rader Hugh Bramblett, is still in practice today.

John Alvin Garrett and his sister Martha Bruton were two of the offspring of John Garrett and Manicy Owings Garrett, who migrated from Laurens, South Carolina. John Alvin Garrett served in the Civil War, was captured at Sevierville, Tennessee, and spent the last part of the war in Rock Island Prison. He married Lou Cox and resided in Forsyth County until his death in 1932 at the age of 90.

Mary Indiana Hawkins Bramblett was born September 13, 1855, died November 13, 1911, and was buried in Friendship Baptist Church's cemetery. She was the daughter of Robert Hawkins and his second wife, Samantha Virginia Brannon Hawkins. She married Dr. Martin Truman Bramblett on April 1, 1874, and they were the parents of nine children: Nora, Jim, Truman, Artie, Rader, Thaddeus, Corbett, Nettie, and Samuel.

Drew Edmond Bennett (born February 29, 1868, and died December 12, 1931) married Kate Little. He owned and operated a grocery and dry goods store in the area where his grandfather Peter Bennett first settled. The community was known as "Drew" for Drew Bennett. The post office, officially established in the community in 1889, was recorded as being located at Drew, Georgia.

Four
County Landmarks

Sawnee Mountain is the highest elevation in Forsyth County at 1,967 feet. Named for Chief Sawnee, a lesser Cherokee chief, the mountain is the subject of numerous stories and legends which have been passed down from generation to generation. Most noted is the tale that Chief Sawnee, too old to go west when the Cherokees were removed, was sealed up with his gold in a cave on the mountain.

Poole's Mill Covered Bridge over Settendown Creek was built after a flood washed away the old bridge in 1900. Started by John Wofford, who abandoned the project, the bridge of town lattice design was completed by Bud Gentry in the early 1900s. It is the only structure in Forsyth County currently on the National Register of Historic Places.

The mill, known through the years for its three owners, has been called Welch's Mill, Scudder's Mill, and Poole's Mill. It featured an overshot waterwheel which powered both a sawmill and gristmill. Located on the banks of Settendown Creek near a covered bridge, the mill served farmers in western Forsyth County for over a century, but the building was burned by vandals in 1947.

Another view of Poole's Mill Bridge shows the structure which was used for first wagons and buggies in its early days and later automobile traffic. Falling into a state of disrepair in 1987, it collapsed into Settendown Creek but was rescued by the board of commissioners and restored for foot traffic only. Today the bridge is part of a county park, which allows visitors to enjoy the scenic area.

The Brannon Hotel, located in Cumming, was operated by Charlie Brannon primarily as a boardinghouse for teachers until 1925 or 1926. Situated just around the corner from Cumming School, it was convenient to both the school and the activities of the town. The hotel was one of the last to remain in operation in Cumming. Although vacant today, the building is still standing.

The building on West Maple Street dubbed the "Old Jail" was originally constructed in 1893. It stood about 230 feet west of the traffic light on the southwest corner of the square. In 1924, it was remodeled, but by the 1940s it was the subject of concern by several grand juries. A new building was erected in the 1980s to replace this structure.

When Forsyth County's first brick courthouse had deteriorated badly, this stately courthouse was proposed to the voters. In 1904, an ad in the *North Georgian* showed this artist's conception of a grandiose building that was to be three stories high. Funds ran short, however, and the building that was constructed looked somewhat different and was only two stories high when finished.

Plans for the second brick courthouse, completed in 1905, had been scaled back. Yet the enthusiasm of the citizens seemed undiminished. The cornerstone ceremony on June 24, 1905, was a day-long event with the Masons from LaFayette Lodge No. 44, F & AM heading the celebration. Col. Hiram Parks Bell, U.S. congressman from Forsyth County, delivered the keynote address and a variety of items were placed inside the cornerstone. Forsyth Countians remained fiercely proud of this building and grieved when it was destroyed by fire on November 5, 1973. Although the interior was completely gutted, county records stored within its vaults were saved.

The walls of the old courthouse were torn away and the void was temporarily filled by trailers which served as county offices while plans were underway to erect a new building. The proposal to rebuild at a site away from the square was not accepted by the voters. After considerable disagreement and bond issues, the present structure was completed and the dedication ceremony took place in 1978.

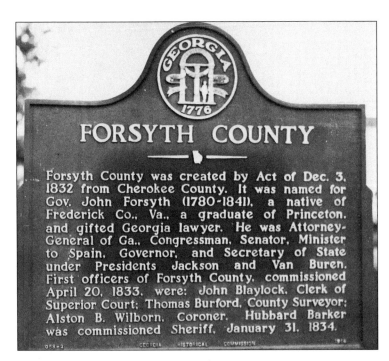

FORSYTH COUNTY

Forsyth County was created by Act of Dec. 3, 1832 from Cherokee County. It was named for Gov. John Forsyth (1780-1841), a native of Frederick Co., Va., a graduate of Princeton, and gifted Georgia lawyer. He was Attorney-General of Ga., Congressman, Senator, Minister to Spain, Governor, and Secretary of State under Presidents Jackson and Van Buren. First officers of Forsyth County, commissioned April 20, 1833, were: John Blaylock, Clerk of Superior Court; Thomas Burford, County Surveyor; Alston B. Wilborn, Coroner. Hubbard Barker was commissioned Sheriff, January 31, 1834.

The historical marker describing the earliest beginnings of Forsyth County was placed on the square before the east facade of the county's second brick courthouse by the Georgia Historical Commission. When the courthouse burned in 1973 and was replaced by the present building, the marker was likewise replaced and moved to its position near the front entrance of the building.

This historical marker, a companion to the marker offering data on early Forsyth County, gives biographical information on Col. William Cumming, for whom the county seat was purportedly named. Although some historians argue that Cumming was named to honor Rev. Frederick Cumming of Wilkes County, the marker has nevertheless remained in place.

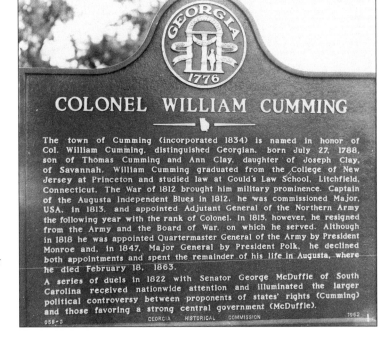

COLONEL WILLIAM CUMMING

The town of Cumming (incorporated 1834) is named in honor of Col. William Cumming, distinguished Georgian, born July 27, 1788, son of Thomas Cumming and Ann Clay, daughter of Joseph Clay, of Savannah. William Cumming graduated from the College of New Jersey at Princeton and studied law at Gould's Law School, Litchfield, Connecticut. The War of 1812 brought him military prominence. Captain of the Augusta Independent Blues in 1812, he was commissioned Major, USA, in 1813, and appointed Adjutant General of the Northern Army the following year with the rank of Colonel. In 1815, however, he resigned from the Army and the Board of War, on which he served. Although in 1818 he was appointed Quartermaster General of the Army by President Monroe and, in 1847, Major General by President Polk, he declined both appointments and spent the remainder of his life in Augusta, where he died February 18, 1863.

A series of duels in 1822 with Senator George McDuffie of South Carolina received nationwide attention and illuminated the larger political controversy between proponents of states' rights (Cumming) and those favoring a strong central government (McDuffie).

The Cumming Band Stand is located on the northeast corner of the courthouse square. It was originally built in the 1890s. The Cumming Cornet Band gave Sunday afternoon concerts from this stand. In later years it has been utilized for a variety of purposes, including choral performances by school groups at Christmas time and oratory from organizations seeking an audience.

This petroglyph was located in the Mount Tabor area of northwest Forsyth County when Rev. George White traveled through the former Cherokee territory in the late 1840s and published his findings in a volume entitled *Historical Collections of Georgia* in 1855. About 1960, it was moved to the University of Georgia at Athens. Efforts have been made over the years to have it returned to Forsyth County.

In the 1900s, Cumming School was housed in the old Hightower Academy building. When first opened in 1888, the school was known as Piedmont College. Then in 1893, it became Hightower Baptist College and shortly thereafter, Hightower Baptist Institute. The board of education established the boundaries for the Cumming School District in 1907 and the title "Cumming Graded School" was applied.

The first and second grade class of Cumming Elementary for the school year 1919–1920 was taught by Mrs. Gussie Tallant. The school continued to be housed in the old Hightower Academy building, with the LaFayette Masonic Lodge Hall on the right end. This portion of the structure was brick and would be used until a new school was erected next door in 1923.

D. F. PULLIAM, Principal

CUMMING ELEMENTARY SCHOOL
Cumming, Georgia

The photo shows Cumming School as it appeared in 1955. Constructed in 1923 adjacent to the old Hightower Baptist Institute, this school burned in 1927 and was rebuilt in a few short months within the same walls. The bricks were handmade at the Cumming brickyard by the school's builder, J.W. Fleming. After the fire of 1927, Fleming and Jim Hughes rebuilt the interior.

The Chattahoochee River has proven to be the most important body of water flowing through the county. During the first half of the nineteenth century, ferries were established at strategic crossings. Then in the 1950s, Buford Dam was constructed and Lake Lanier was flooded in 1957. Today the river is a source of drinking water, and Lake Lanier maintains flood control and provides recreation for North Georgians.

Pictured is Lake Sidney Lanier with a view of Sawnee Mountain in the background. Named for Georgia poet Sidney Lanier, the lake project became a reality in the 1950s after years of political maneuvering, planning, and construction efforts. Cemeteries and significant structures, such as the Vann Tavern, were moved to higher ground prior to the flooding of the lake in 1957. Bridges across the area, such as Brown's Bridge on Highway 369 and the two bridges on Highway 53 were built.

Buford Dam, which creates the lake, is an earthen dam containing a powerhouse for generating electricity. The floodgates and generating process are now controlled from Carter's Lake. Lake Sidney Lanier is maintained by the U.S. Army Corps of Engineers and is one of the most popular North Georgia recreation sites, attracting thousands of visitors annually.

Five

Citizens
Great and Small

Dr. Louis Orr, who was born in the Redd House in Cumming, later became president of the American Medical Association. On November 4, 1959, Dr. Orr accepted an invitation to return to Cumming and address a meeting of the Chattahoochee Medical Society. Pictured left to right are Dr. Marcus Mashburn Sr., Dr. Louis M. Orr, Mrs. Orr, and Dr. D.C. Kelly.

The Otwell family has produced several members who have served Cumming and Forsyth County in various official capacities. Here, James A. Otwell III is pictured with his father, James A. Otwell Jr., when the elder Otwell was serving as Forsyth County's representative in the Georgia Legislature. James A. Otwell Jr. was Forsyth's representative in 1951–1952 and 1953–1954.

Roy P. Otwell Sr. was Forsyth County's representative to the Georgia Legislature from 1959 through 1962. Otwell was a prominent businessman of Cumming, serving as president of the Bank of Cumming, operating the Ford dealership, and engaging in numerous other enterprises. It was through his leadership after the Great Depression that the poultry industry prospered and thus improved the standard of living for the county.

Dr. Marcus Mashburn Sr. represented the county in the State Legislature in 1949–1950 and again in 1955–1956. He also served as the mayor of Cumming in 1917 and again in 1961–1966. Born in Cumming on October 7, 1890, he married Mary Katherine Summerour on April 26, 1916, and later Kate Rhodes. He was the state senator for the 51st District in 1929–1931, and for the 33rd District 1951–1952 and 1957–1958. While in public office, Dr. Mashburn supported the oxidation pond for the City of Cumming and the Buford Dam and Lake Lanier Projects, deeded land for Cumming City Park and City Hall, and received recognition for his years on the board of education when Mashburn School was named in his honor. He was of the Methodist faith. Dr. Mashburn died December 7, 1978, and was laid to rest in Cumming Cemetery. His two sons, Dr. Marcus Mashburn Jr. and Dr. James 'Jim" Mashburn, practiced medicine in Forsyth County throughout their careers.

The postmaster, clerks, and carriers of the Cumming Post Office pictured here, from left to right, are Ed Puett (postmaster), Joe Patterson, Kirby Kemp, Hiram Kelly, Webster Shadburn, Albert Pruitt, Bob Hope, Homer Hyde, Bill Pool, Olen Merritt, and Oscar Hyde. The small post offices of the county were closed when Rural Free Delivery began and mail was delivered from Cumming.

Forsyth County's post office clerks in 1928 were William Pool, Major Nuckolls, Dewitt Jones, Oscar Hyde (front), Homer Hyde, and Gordon Hyde. A list of Cumming postmasters from the records of Ray Taylor indicate that Augustus C. Kennemore, not pictured, was commissioned postmaster on April 1, 1928, and served until February 22, 1934, when Kirby A. Kemp filled the office.

Dr. Hiram P. Riden (1831–1906) is pictured with Clark, his caretaker. In addition to his medical practice, Dr. Riden was a petitioner and subscriber for Piedmont College in 1888 and was listed as a member of the board of directors of that institution. Moreover, he was listed in the Cumming District in the *Planters and Farmers Gazetteer* of 1888–1889 and in the Big Creek District as a physician.

Dr. Martin Truman Bramblett, in buggy, is pictured in front of his office on Bramblett Road with three of his sons: Dr. Rader Hugh Bramblett, Dr. Joel Thaddeus Bramblett, and William Corbett Bramblett. The horses are Mag and Meg. Dr. Martin T. Bramblett was the eldest of three generations of Bramblett physicians to practice in the county. His son, Dr. Rader Hugh, was followed by his grandson, Dr. Rupert Harold Bramblett.

Benjamin Perry Roper (1868–1943) was the son of Claborn Thompson Roper and Martha Tallant Roper. A businessman, Ben Roper owned and officiated as president of the Bank of Cumming, ran a cotton gin, served as postmaster of Cuba, Georgia, from December 22, 1902, until October 17, 1903, and operated a general store, where he was murdered in 1943.

Ben Roper is pictured with his wife, Maggie Tribble Roper, the daughter of Newton and Canzada Sams Tribble, in front of his store in the Cuba settlement. The couple resided next to the store building in an impressive Victorian home featuring ornate gingerbread trim, a wraparound porch, and a double sunburst in the front gable. Ben and Maggie Roper are buried in Friendship's cemetery.

Toy Settle (left), the last of the Settle family to occupy the old homeplace at Shakerag, is pictured with Junior Samples of TV fame. The eldest son of Alvin and Odessa Bullock Samples, Junior Samples was born in Forsyth County on August 10, 1926. Before achieving national fame on Hee Haw, his occupation might have been listed as a maker of "white lightning."

Dr. W.P. Ezzard, a native Forsyth Countian, is shown examining the muscles of Ezzard Charles, NBA World Heavyweight Champion, when Charles visited the physician in Lawrenceville. Dr. Ezzard, who practiced medicine for decades in Lawrenceville, was the physician when Ezzard Charles, his namesake, was born. Incidentally, Dr. Ezzard brought over 3,000 babies into the world during his career.

James Madison Vaughan typifies the traditional Forsyth County farmer, as he is pictured here with his mule. He was a descendent of James and Susan Vaughan, who migrated from Henry County, Virginia, to Spartanburg, South Carolina. The Vaughan family played an important role in the development of Haw Creek Baptist Church, which was constituted in 1841.

Isaac Wesley "Philo" Bagley and Fannie Jones Bagley are pictured in the yard of their homeplace. I.W. Bagley is listed as a disabled Confederate pensioner who served in Company I, 16th Georgia Regiment and lost an arm on May 3, 1863, at Chancellorsville, Virginia. He was a member of Shiloh Church and was listed on the church roll of 1900–1920.

Florence Garrett Chapman is captured here in a dress which exemplifies the height of fashion. A descendent of the Garrett family whose ancestors migrated to Forsyth County from Virginia via Laurens, South Carolina, Florence Garrett apparently married before arriving in Forsyth County. She is listed as a member of Shiloh Methodist Church prior to 1909 and again in 1900–1920.

Jessie Garrett, who later married Clinton Higgins, is pictured with her mother, Louiza Cox Garrett. Born March 15, 1895, Jessie was the youngest child of John Alvin Garrett, a Civil War soldier, and Lou Cox Garrett, who was the daughter of Sim and Louiza Gilbert Cox. Subsequent to her marriage, Jessie Garrett Higgins moved to Atlanta, where she resided until her death.

Rupert and Ruth Bramblett, children of Dr. Rader Hugh and Ida Palestine Garrett Bramblett, were the subject of a traveling photographer about 1919. Rupert, born September 6, 1918, later became a physician, and his sister Ruth, born April 12, 1910, married Clyde Bannister. Both children in the photograph continue to reside in Forsyth County.

In the 1920s, Rupert Bramblett looked forward to visits from his grandfather John Alvin Garrett, who would relate Civil War stories. Garrett would sit ramrod straight atop his mule as he made the trek from the Frogtown community to visit his kinfolks near Pleasant Grove. Garrett continued his visits, even as he reached an advanced age. He died in 1932 and was buried in Friendship Baptist Church's cemetery.

Six

Kinfolks

The McAfee family in 1865 included, from left to right, as follows: James Melville McAfee, Margaret Emily McAfee, Ruth Avaline McAfee, Ann Reynolds McAfee, Mary Ann McAfee, Martha Jane McAfee (the great-granddaughter of Robert M. Richardson Sr.), Sarah Louise McAfee, and Rev. John Whitaker McAfee, who came to Georgia from Buncomb County, North Carolina, about 1830.

Claud and his wife, Maudie Phillips Groover, resided in Forsyth County until about 1923. Claud was the son of William J. and Judah Kelly Groover. During his youth, Claud Groover played in the Cumming Band, which gave concerts from the bandstand on the courthouse square, and was captain of the Cumming baseball team in 1889–1900. In 1925, this couple moved to Toccoa, where Claud Groover operated the Ford dealership.

T. Sylvester Tallant (born on March 7, 1878, and died September 14, 1940) married Mary J. "Mollie" Garrett (born on April 25, 1876, and died November 25, 1953). She was the daughter of John Alvin Garrett. Both are buried in Friendship Baptist Church cemetery. Their seven children were as follows: Mattie, William M., Ebb, Anna Lou, Ruby Mae, Morris, and Elvira.

The Harrison Tallant family, photographed in the front yard of the family dwelling, included, from left to right, the following: (front row) Ezra Tallant, Harrison Tallant (seated), baby Leila Grace Tallant (in lap), Landrum Tallant, Delila Maiden Hurt Tallant (seated), and Annie Jane Tallant; (second row) Joel Tallant and Gertrude Tallant.

The William T. Hunter family was photographed in 1911. Five sons became doctors or dentists. Seated are Mr. and Mrs. William T. Hunter (the parents). Standing are, from left to right, Dr. John T. Hunter, Dr. Joseph P. Hunter, William Gordon Hunter, Dr. Robert I. Hunter, Cordelia Ann Hunter Devore, George E. Hunter, Mattie Hunter Cannon, Dr. Edmund Hunter, and Dr. Ancil L. Hunter.

The family of Robert G. and Rosannah Clayton Holbrook was photographed in 1895. They are, from left to right, as follows: (first row) Fannie Holbrook, Robert G., Thomas, Rosannah Holbrook, Alfred Holbrook, and Theora Holbrook; (second row) Mary Holbrook, Ida Holbrook, Agnes Holbrook, unidentified (possibly the wife of James), and James Holbrook.

The Augustus L. Glover family is featured in this yardscape. (Augustus Glover is also pictured in Chapter 2 driving a mule and wagon.) From left to right are Doll Glover, Docky Glover, Gordon Glover, Evaline Venable Glover, baby Mary (?), and Augustus L. Glover. The 1900 U.S. Census of Forsyth County indicates that Augustus L. Glover was residing in Big Creek District.

The three sons of Joseph Gaither Puett are William Wesley Puett, Joseph Glenn Puett, and Garnett McAfee Puett. The boys' father, Joseph Gaither Puett, married Sallie L. McAfee on October 5, 1882, in Forsyth County. Joseph G. Puett was commissioned postmaster of Cumming District in 1889. Garnett Mack Puett was listed as a farmer in 1886.

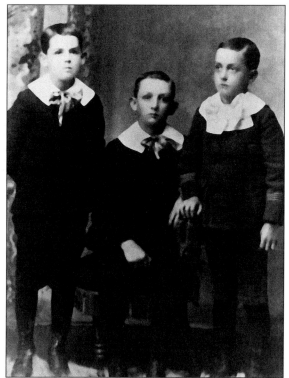

The Clarence C. "Dolly" Bagley family, including Clarence C. Bagley, Garland Bagley, Blanch Bagley, and Creola Bagley, are pictured in front of their beautiful home in the Sharon community. The Bagley's third child, Marie, would be born later. Garland Bagley is the historian who amassed the collection of photographs featured in this book.

Members of the William Royston Otwell family are, from left to right, as follows: (first row) Mrs. Benjamin (Jane) Otwell, Roy P. Otwell, Toy Otwell, Myrtie Otwell, Mae Otwell, George Ingram, Chesley Otwell, and baby Ivan Otwell; (second row) Dr. Jim Otwell, Arthur Otwell, William Royston Otwell, Sallie Otwell Ingram, Ann Pilgrim Otwell, and Izzie Chamblee Otwell.

The sons of James Lumpkin Heard and Martha Parlee Hudlow Heard are pictured in front of the Heard Store at Frogtown about 1897. From left to right, they are George Lumpkin Heard, John Pinckney Heard, Seymore Heard, James Linton Heard, Walker Heard, Arthur Heard, and Charlie Heard. The general store business was a tradition among the Heards.

In addition to being a minister, Rev. J.W.H. Robertson was a whaler as well. His family is pictured here, from left to right, as follows: (first row) Ingram, Marie, Sherman, and Furman; (second row) John, J.W. Hill, Martha, Berthan, and Bessie; (last row) Minnie, who later was the mother of Earl R. Bramblett, who rose to the level of vice president of General Motors in Detroit.

The George Bagwell family was captured on film in front of the Bagwell home, which would later be the site of Oak Grove School, started in 1870. Family members include, from left to right, George Bagwell with Buren Bagwell in his lap, Ober Bagwell, Mrs. Bagwell with Nubie Bagwell in her lap, and Dessie Bagwell.

The W.J. Groover family included, from left to right, the following: (first row) Virginia Groover, Nettie Lewis Groover, Charles Tillman Martin, Virgil Martin, Mary Groover, Willie Mae Martin, Frank Groover, and Eliff Martin; (second row) Maude G. Phillips Groover, Claudia Green Groover, Ola Groover Martin, Sarah Caine Groover, and Sarah Simmons Groover; (back row) William Claud Groover, Walter Groover, Milton Martin, Marshall Groover, Myrtie Groover, Lorens Groover, William Jacob Groover, and Cornelius Groover.

The Pendleton Holbrooks pictured here are, from left to right, as follows: (front row) Myrtle Holbrook, Ruby Holbrook Hammond, Cora Lee Holbrook, Hoyt Holbrook (baby), J. Pendleton Holbrook, Louie Holbrook, Daisy Holbrook, and Mary Holbrook Bramblett; (second row) Bessie Haygood Holbrook, Lover Holbrook, Jean Haygood Barrett, Paul Holbrook, Edith Haygood Bramblett, and Grady Bramblett.

The Rawleigh Echols group includes, from left to right, the following: (first row) Audry, Jake, Raleigh Wilson, Dossie Thomas, Margaret, Thelma, and Evelyn; (second row) Leslie Ralph, Donald Echols in lap, James Coy in lap, J.C. Raleigh Wilson, Lilly Major Echols, Ruby Mae, Grace Gilbert Echols with Clifford in lap; (third row) Raleigh Winford, Ruby Day Echols, Beatrice Bagley Echols, Hannah Echols Yarbrough, Major Cliff, James Euell Echols, Sam P. Thomas, and Herman Gaston.

The James Euell Echols family was photographed at a reunion on Fort Street in Atlanta, Georgia. From left to right, family members include Ralph Echols, Lester Echols, Homer Echols, Claude Echols, Dossie L. Echols, Raleigh Echols, Charlie Echols, Perry Echols, Hardy Echols, James Echols, Euell Echols, Hannah Jane Blackstock Echols, Fannie Echols, Senoria Echols, and Jessie Echols.

In the front yard of the George Olivet homeplace are its owner, George Olivet, and Selena Olivet, Jancy Olivet, and Amanda Olivet. George Olivet, like most other Forsyth Countians, was a farmer by occupation. A photograph of him plowing his mule is included in Chapter 9 of this book, entitled "Country Living."

The Seymour Heard family resided at Frogtown in northwest Forsyth County. Seymour Heard was the son of James Lumpkin Heard. The photograph of this family identifies those pictured as Seymour and LaVada Heard (adults) and Carter and Jeff (children). Carter, however, may be incorrectly named, for she is definitely a young lady (Nancy Lee or Vada Lou?).

Seven
Home Sweet Home

Dr. Ansel Strickland's home was located on Kelly Mill Road on the west side of Cumming. Near the turn of the century, a picket fence surrounded the property which, in addition to the fine white house, enclosed Dr. Strickland's office building and a windmill for his scientific experiments. In recent years, Cumming mayor Ford Gravitt's family has resided in the house.

The Samuel Spence home is purportedly the oldest brick house in Forsyth County. The bricks were handmade. Still standing in the early 1980s, the house was located on Land Lot 1222 in the Second District, First Section of the county. State Highway 141 currently runs through this land lot, which is located in the southern part of the county near the Fulton County line.

This impressive structure housed the Abijah Julian family. Born December 12, 1842, Abijah John Julian married Minnie A. Bailey, an educator and daughter of Dr. Samuel S. Bailey and Julia Ann Thompson Bailey, on April 19, 1864 in Alabama, where their families had refuged during the Civil War. Abijah Julian served with the Kellogg Rifles in the Confederate Army.

The Thomas J. Pirkle home was located in Cumming. Thomas Jefferson Pirkle (born June 30, 1866, and died October 14, 1945) married Clara Abigail Patterson on December 26, 1894. He was admitted as a freshman at Piedmont College in 1892. In 1912, this residence was #17 in the Cumming telephone book. Thomas J. Pirkle and his wife are both buried in Cumming Cemetery.

The Eliza Chatham Bagley home place was on the Big Creek–Alpharetta Road when she served as postmistress at Big Creek, Georgia. Eliza Bagley later went to live with her daughter Ellen in Shrive, Texas, where she is interred. Her husband, Francis Marion Bagley, was killed in the Civil War.

The Terry-Settle House is likely the oldest home in Forsyth County to be lived in continually until recent years. Built in 1838 or 1839, the house has undergone several additions and renovations. A succession of land owners for Land Lot 1079 on which the structure is located began with William Alley, who drew the lot in the 1832 Gold Lottery. John G. Terry married Elizabeth Cawley, its owner in 1866. It passed next to Martin Terry and then through another

succession of owners. In 1892, George Thomas Settle and his wife, Sarah Cottrell Settle, purchased the property. Sarah was the granddaughter of Martin Terry. Hence the name Terry-Settle House was established. The historic home on Southers Circle is currently a part of the Old Atlanta Club and is being rehabilitated by its current owners.

The Hiram P. Bell House, located at the intersection of Kelly Mill Road and the present state Highway 20, was the residence of one of Forsyth County's most prominent citizens. Colonel Bell was a local lawyer, Mason, Confederate soldier, delegate to the Georgia Secession Convention, state senator, representative to the Second Confederate Congress, and U.S. congressman for the terms 1863–1865 and 1877–1880.

The E.C. McAfee home in Cumming, built around 1842, sat atop the ridge outside the city limits on a farm on the east side of Cumming. When Highway 400 was constructed, the slave cabins behind the house were destroyed. Then in the 1980s the house was burned as practice for the fire department. E.C. McAfee, a prominent businessman, was the son of John Whitaker McAfee.

The Will and Stella Benson Bell home, still in excellent condition, was built in the Chestatee community on Highway 306 (Keith Bridge Road). The youngest daughter of Washington and Sarah A. Benson, Stella Benson Bell was born near Cumming in 1889. She became a teacher, civic leader, and outstanding pianist, and held the distinction of being the first woman in Forsyth County to drive an automobile.

The Bryan Redd house is situated on the west side of Cumming at the intersection of Highway 20 and Kelly Mill Road. It was originally the John Hudson home. Dr. Louis M. Orr, a renowned Florida urologist born in this house, later became president of the American Medical Association. In 1959, Dr. Orr returned to Cumming to meet with the local medical society.

The home of Dr. Marcus Mashburn Sr. was located on the east side of Dahlonega Street to the north of Cumming. A distinguished physician, Dr. Mashburn practiced medicine in Cumming for decades. He converted the Mashburn Hotel on the square to a hospital for expectant mothers and later established it as the Mary Alice Hospital. Dr. Mashburn married Mary Katherine Summerour and later, Kate Rhodes.

One of Forsyth County's oldest homes, the Stephen Clement House was built near Big Creek, or "Wildcat," as the community was called. Just visible at the end of the porch, Stephen Guy Clement (1880–1966) was the son of William Clement (born 1836) and the grandson of Stephen Clement (born in 1807 in Anderson County, South Carolina). Stephen G. Clement married Essie Nally.

Junior Samples resided in this house when he told a "fish tale" that ultimately led to his role on the Hee Haw television program. Prior to his discovery, A.J. "Junior" Samples worked part time in the pulpwood business, but the production of white lightning could be considered his occupation as well. Samples's talent for storytelling boosted his rise to stardom.

The James Bettis homeplace was located on the road running west from Bethlehem Baptist Church in the western section of Forsyth County. In 1876, Bettis was one of the petitioners who were seeking the construction of a road leaving the Atlanta and Gilmer's Ferry Road and passing the residences of Charlotte Vickery, Bettis, F.M. Holbrook, and others.

The Eli Davis house on Tribble Gap Road across from the Bank of Cumming was one of the oldest homes in the town of Cumming before it was demolished several years ago. Davis (1845–1945) married Frances E. Merritt in 1867. He was listed as a farmer when his son, Thomas, attended Hightower Baptist Institute in 1893. Eli and Frances Davis are buried in Cumming Cemetery.

Mrs. Creola Scales Bagley is pictured at her home in 1958. She was the widow of Clarence "Dolly" Bagley and the mother of Garland C., Blanche, and Marie. The house still stands in the Sharon community in southern Forsyth County. Garland Bagley, who amassed the collection of photographs used in this book, was raised in this homeplace.

Eight

Historic Churches and Early Ministers

Silver Springs Baptist Church was one of the oldest churches in Forsyth County. The exact date it was constituted is unknown. However, it was already in existence on Land Lot 241 in the 14th District, First Section when the Hightower Baptist Association was formed in 1835. The cemetery where this church was located has no markers, only fieldstones.

Pleasant Grove Methodist Church was chartered in 1871 from the membership of Cool Springs and Andrew's Chapel Methodist Churches. Incomplete church records indicate that Rev. J.N. Myer served as pastor in 1874. The present sanctuary was erected in 1928 with Grady Bramblett as chairman of the building committee. The building was remodeled in 1957.

Ebenezer Methodist Church, located 7 miles northeast of Cumming on present-day Highway 369, was established around 1834. The church began independently and was not sponsored by another church. The Mashburns were among the charter members. Minutes do not exist from 1840 to 1878. Erected in 1875, the structure in use today is the third church building on the site.

Several members of the Mashburn family became preachers in Forsyth County, including Rev. J. Harvey Mashburn, pictured here. Alfred M. Pierce described the work of these Forsyth County preachers as follows: "The local preachers continued to pursue their ordinary business, but, having in their hearts an experience that urged to be told, they gave themselves to the work of the ministry on Sundays."

Bethlehem Baptist Church was constituted in 1836 with 13 charter members: David Talant, Odean Castleberry, Elijah Davis, James Davis, Nathan Pool, Thomas W. Williams, Sarah Tallant, Mary Davis, Lucinda Davis, Nancy Bentley, Frances Chappelier, Margaret Poole, and Mary Ann Williams. The presbytery was composed of Revs. Solomon Peek, Richard Phillips, and Peter Kuykendall.

Sharon Baptist Church was constituted on July 16, 1846, with Rev. F.M. Hawkins, Rev. Burrell Higgins, and Thomas Rogers (deacon), forming the presbytery. Eighteen charter members were recorded. Early officers were Joseph H. Williams (moderator) and Thomas Rogers (clerk). Rev. Joseph H. Williams was called as supply. For over 46 years, F.M. Hawkins served as pastor.

Cross Roads Baptist Church was organized in 1865. The first church, a log building, was located near Major Tinsley's. The second church is a brick structure now in use. Early records of Cross Roads were destroyed. Rev. Jesse Sherfield organized the first Sunday school and served as pastor. Some of the earliest known preachers include Rev. Robb Conner, Rev. George Barnewell, and Rev. Tommy Robison.

On February 8, 1913, John Sorrells called together a group of people to organize a church in southern Forsyth County. The church was named Brookwood in honor of Mr. and Mrs. William Brooks, who had lived nearby and wished for a church in the community. The presbytery consisted of Rev. V.V. Braddy with deacons John Sorrells, G.W. Bagwell, and Edgar Anderson. There were 23 charter members.

These ministers who attended the Oak Grove Ordination in 1910–1912 are, from left to right, as follows: (first row) Revs. Josiah Bannister, J.L. Wyatt, J.R. Stone, J.J. Dempsey, Will Thomas, and unidentified; (second row) Revs. John Smith, three unidentified men, Jim Kelley, J.W. Parks, and Eli Sherrill; (third row) Revs. Luke Burgess, Simp Bailey, Jesse Marion Corn, and Thad Pickett.

The presbytery for Zion Hill Baptist Church, organized in 1881, included the following: Rev. F.M. Hawkins (moderator), Rev. W.J. Hyde, Rev. W.F. Wofford, Rev. J.B. Wallis, Rev. W.J. Pirkle, J.A. Hope, W.W. Harris, A.J. Logan, Rev. S.L. Hayes, Rev. G.B. Sewell, and E. Hope. W.J. Hyde was elected supply for 1881–1882, and T.J. Reese was named the church clerk.

Established in 1833, Mount Tabor has the distinction of being the oldest church in present-day Forsyth County. The church was constituted at a meeting at Dennis Carroll's with Reverend Reeves and Reverend Manning in attendance. There were 12 charter members. On January 25, 1847, George Cockburn gave 4 acres in Land Lot 159 in the Third District, First Section for a new church.

Longstreet Baptist Church was established in 1911 with the following individuals serving as the presbytery: Rev. L.H. Burgess, Rev. R.A. Roper, Rev. S.L. Hays, D.W. Boling (deacon), D.W. DeVore (secretary), and E.L. Nix (deacon). The land for Longstreet School was given in 1883 by Mrs. Whittier, grandmother of Grady Puckett. The school was used for services until a church building could be constructed.

Organized in 1843, Salem Baptist Church began with Drewery Hutchins as first pastor and 12 charter members: John Henderson, Mary Henderson, Hannah Watson, Keziah Mauldin, William Stovall, Mary Stovall, John Burris, Lucinda Burris, Mary Jane Burris, Mary Owen, Elizabeth Owen, and Betsey Ann Owen. In 1847, John Gazaway donated 5 acres for a church and cemetery site.

Rev. John E. "Jackie" Rieves was born in Chatham, North Carolina, in 1802. His great-grandfather, Thomas, immigrated from England. His grandfather and father, both named Thomas, were natives of Dunwoody County, Virginia. Jackie was the fifth child in a family of ten. He married Elizabeth Warren in 1824 and lived near Yellow Creek Church. He pastored Salem and Bethel Baptist Churches early in their history.

Beaver Ruin Baptist Church was established June 6, 1835, at a meeting at a schoolhouse on Young Deer Creek. Serving as the presbytery were Rev. H. Posey, Rev. R. Phillips, Edmond Bagby, W. Hammond, and Ausborn Haygood. The church began as "Young Deers Creek," but the name was changed to Beaver Ruin in August of 1835. The first church building was burned by Native Americans.

Bethel Baptist Church was organized on February 6, 1836, and the presbytery consisted of Revs. Richard Phillips, William Mears, and Drury Hutchins and deacons Osburn Haygood and Joseph Hammond. In 1836, the church was incorporated by the Georgia Legislature. A. Thornton and G.B. Light sold 2.5 acres for the church in 1843.

Rev. Humphery Posey was born in Henry County, Virginia, in 1780 and spent his youth in Burke County. He married Lettice Jolly and then Mrs. Jane Stokes of Newnan, Georgia. Posey was considered a great preacher among those who preached at the Georgia Baptist Convention. He died in 1846 after preaching his last sermon at Ebenezer Church in Coweta County.

Rev. John Webb has been identified as a Baptist minister at Cumming, Georgia. He may be the same John Webb listed on the 1834 State Census of Forsyth County or the John Webb who owned a farm in the Antioch school district in 1907. A John W. Webb (1869–1936) is buried in Beaver Ruin Cemetery.

Rev. Jesse M. Wood, editor of the *Baptist Banner* in Cumming, was born in Elbert County, Georgia, in 1815. He married Eliza P. Milner of Pike County in 1846, and they moved around the state as Reverend Wood preached and served as leader of several Baptist academies. Active in the Cherokee Baptist Convention in the late 1850s, Wood then moved from Rome to Newnan to Atlanta and on to Cumming in 1880.

Nine
Country Living

Clearing the land and tilling the soil was a way of life in rural Forsyth County. By mule, horse, or ox power, the land was cleared with little concern for soil erosion and run-off. Spring planting was done "by the signs," and, in fall, remains from the crops were turned under after fodder was stored. Pictured here, George Olivet is seen plowing his fields, using his mule.

Flora Olivet Freeland was photographed as she picked cotton in the early fall. Cotton was the cash crop of the Forsyth County farmers and remained so until prices fell during the Depression and people turned to raising poultry for survival. Cotton was planted in the spring, "chopped" during the summer, and harvested by hand in the fall. Even the scrap cotton was saved after the main crop had been picked.

Justice of the Peace courthouses were scattered throughout the county to enable citizens to transact simple matters without making the difficult trek into Cumming over dusty or muddy roads. These buildings served as polling places as well. The structure pictured here is the Justice of the Peace Courthouse of the Big Creek Militia District (#795).

Hardy Strickland's corn crib is an example of one of the outbuildings found on most farms. Corn remained in the field and was harvested during a dry time after frost. First it was pulled from the stalks and thrown into heaps. Then it was hauled to the barnyard and shucked. And, finally, it was thrown into the crib and the shucks were put in the shuck house.

Wherever there were people, there were chickens. Eggs were eaten almost daily. Chicken houses did not exist in the early days, as chickens roamed free and roosted in trees. In inclement weather they might take shelter under the house, which likely was not underpinned. It was quite an undertaking to keep up with where the hens were laying, but a necessary task if the family was to have eggs.

The Etowah River west of Frogtown was important to the farmers during pioneer times. Its rapid waters provided a source of fish to supplement the usual diet. Livestock, too, enjoyed its pure water. And when power to operate a mill was needed, it was at hand for residents of the area. Then as now, the Etowah River was one of the most scenic spots in the county.

A lone chimney in a rural setting signified that the area had once been a homeplace, such as this site of the Blackstock home. Chimney building and well digging were considered professions. Some of the chimneys constructed with red clay mud lasted over a hundred years. Most chimneys and fireplaces were made of logs and rocks held together with this red clay mixture.

Buice's Store in the Sharon community is typical of the general merchandise business in every community. Although farms were mostly self-sufficient, nevertheless, a few items had to be purchased. The local store met those needs. For example, women bought the kinds of cloth that couldn't be made at home: jeans, hickory shirting, calico, gingham, flannel, and ducking.

As the agrarian population increased, livestock began to be confined in pastures, such as the one in this photo taken in southern Forsyth County. In the early days there was no stock law, so fields for crops were fenced in and animals roamed free. Farmers designated Sundays as the time to check on their livestock and to brand the newborns as they were discovered.

This mill on Daves Creek has a history in the community from the time of the Cherokees. It was built by Dave Cordery, a Native American, and later owned by Charles Vickery, also a Cherokee. Then the white settlers took over and it became known as the Jim Terry Mill. When it was sold again, it became the Joe Buice Grist Mill.

The Fanny Harrell cabin was the first structure erected by Edward Harrell when his family migrated around 1835 to the western Forsyth County area, where he would later establish a thriving plantation. Edward Harrell died in California and his son Newton gained ownership of the land. Subsequent to Newton Harrell's death, his daughter Fanny moved from the fine house back to the original cabin.

Next to bread, meat—especially pork—was the most important food of the pioneers. Hog killing time arrived with cold weather when the moon was right. The hog was killed, scalded to remove the hair, gutted, and finally cut up and put away, usually in a smokehouse where it was salted down. When the insides of the hog were removed, the fat was taken from the guts and rendered into lard, as seen here. By the old wash pot method, the lard was boiled outside in an iron pot over an open fire. The guts were cleaned and made into chitlins or soap grease. The children enjoyed playing with the hog bladder, which was washed and blown up to make a balloon. When the entire process was complete, two hams, two shoulders, and two middlings composed the main parts, with the head and feet being made into sauce and the liver and lights, into liver mush. Fresh meat was usually shared with the neighbors.

Tom Crow's Store in the Oscarville community furnished needed supplies for the farm families in the nearby countryside. Oscarville was located near present-day Highway 369 and in fairly close proximity to Lake Lanier. Pictured here, from left to right, in the early 1930s are Kenneth Crow, Floy Crow, Sue Crow, Faustine Reynolds, and Blondine Reynolds.

In a typical rural scene, Lettie Ann Smith Westbrook is feeding chickens in the yard of her home. Adding to the pioneer appearance of the homeplace are the wooden shingles on the house, the two-over-two windows, and the well shelter. The house is not underpinned and fieldstones are used for steps. The yard is "swept," as lawns were not a part of the farm setting.

Ten
Schools and Scholars

Before the state provided funds for schools, local citizens assumed the responsibility. Teachers would traverse the community to sign up parents who agreed to send a certain number of students for a certain number of days. Pupils attended five days a week. Mount Zion School, pictured about 1921, was a better than average building with a sizable group of students for that time period.

This photograph of Bethlehem High School was taken September 4, 1895, at the school building in western Forsyth County. The term "high school" was used to indicate that the older and more advanced students were in attendance, as well as those who would today be classified as "primary" and "elementary."

Students at Gravel Springs School were captured on film on August 17, 1903. Although the teacher's name is illegible, the assistant was Miss Jimmie Kemp. The families represented by the pupils included Robinson, Strickland, Hall, Buice, Settle, Gilbert, Burgess, Terry, Robinson, Bagley, Rogers, Brooks, Williams, Christopher, Moulder, and others.

Pearl Gober was the teacher of Cross Roads Schools in 1906–1907. Pupils who attended were from the following families: Hammond, Bennett, Burdett, Whitmire, Martin, Chastain, Mathis, Cain, Hughes, Smith, Gazaway, Morgan, Elliott, Godfrey, Nalley, Free, and Higgins. Several families had multiple students enrolled in various grades and academic levels.

At Harris Grove School in 1908, Vinner Brady was the teacher and Arbin Hall, the assistant. Families represented included the following: Bagley, Hainey, Pettyjohn, Green, Higgins, Spence, Allen, Vaughan, Echols, Harris, McWhorter, Sorrells, Comer, Brooks, and Pritchard. The Bagley and Allen families enrolled five pupils each, with the Haineys running a close second with four youngsters enrolled.

In 1934, Itley School was located near Pleasant View Baptist Church. From left to right, the pupils were as follows: (front row) Ansel Goss, Bobby McGinnis, Marie Porter, Dessie Goss, unidentified, Annie Lou Fagan, Aline Glover, Margaret Bagley, Harold McGinnis, and Edwin Bales; (middle row) Preston Bagley, unidentified, Katherine Glover, Sybil Strickland, Alvin Brannon, Erin Barnett, Virgil Brannon, and Fred Stripland; (last row) Ellen Brannon, Marie Bagwell, Lelia Bell Glover, Lora Mae Bagley, Behre Bagwell, Joe Brannon, Leonard Barnett, C.W. Phillips, and Ronald Bagley.

Cumming Graded School was housed in the old Piedmont College building, later called the Hightower Baptist College and Hightower Baptist Institute (1893). Education in Cumming in 1910 was a partnership with LaFayette Lodge and the Cumming School District. The Masons owned the building and retained a section for their lodge activities. The classrooms were rented out for educational purposes.

At Oak Grove School in 1915, Arbin Hall served as principal and Reno Green as assistant. Oak Grove was one of the larger rural schools, drawing its pupils from the following families: Payne, Haney, Murdock, Fagan, Holmes, Brannon, Streetman, Homes, Bagwell, Bagley, Hansard, King, Scott, Boling, Purcell, Thompson, Gibson, Boles, Nuckolls, Jackson, Murdock, and Nalley.

Mount Zion School, located near present-day Highway 369 in northeast Forsyth County, served students from the Green, Watson, Bennett, Crow, Durand, Dover, Jordan, Mathis, Olivet, Mayfield, Murphy, Hale, Hemphill, Kennemore, Reed, Ledbetter, Bonds, Smith, Bryson, and Booker families. The school building, pictured on page 97, was a fine structure for the educational setting of its day.

Floy Hill was the teacher of Settendown School in 1918. Currently, Settendown Road runs from Highway 369 a short distance from the Coal Mountain intersection over to Highway 400. In 1918, however, the school knew no paved road. The pupils of that era were from these families: Bolton, Bennett, Norrell, Martin, Willard, Gravitt, Lamb, Akins, Carnes, Smith, Bolton, Wilbanks, and Willard.

About 1925, Spot School existed in the Spot community, which was between Friendship and Coal Mountain. The road through the area now goes from Bramblett Road to Highway 9. Located near the foot of Sawnee Mountain's northern range, Spot School drew students from the following families: Heard, Pilcher, McCoy, Martin, McBrayer, Vernon, Pirkle, Williams, Vance, Wallace, Worley, Tallant, and Hicks.

This photograph of the Coal Mountain School group was taken in 1928. The old Coal Mountain School was closed around 1953, but in 1981 a new building in the community, also called Coal Mountain School, was opened to house approximately 520 students. The original school drew from the Heard, Wallis, Martin, Smith, Pendley, Reese, Pilgrim, Hooper, and other families in the area.

Chestatee High School was located in the northern part of the county on the road now referred to as Keith Bridge (Highway 306). This fine brick building, constructed around 1931, has served students to the present time. The wooden gym on the right of the photograph has been torn away and renovations have recently made the school's facade unrecognizable from the building in the picture.

Center Grove School, photographed about 1926, was located on Jot'em Down Road in the Chestatee community. Consolidated with Chestatee High School, Center Grove closed in 1931 and students moved into the new brick structure on Keith Bridge Road. As frequently happened in the rural schools of the county, the property on which the school stood reverted back to its original owner or owners, who happened to be Alonzo and Alice Pendley. According to an article in the *Forsyth County News*, the empty building was used as a dwelling house and later as a chicken house. Then in 1956 or 1957, it was demolished by Herbert Martin, who used

the lumber to build a garage. Some of the older students in 1926 included Ray Hemphill, Forrest Martin, Easter Lee Mayfield, Hoyt Stanford, Verna Strickland, Ralph Westbrooks, Glenn Mathis, Walter Howard, Ray Howard, Barney Pendley, Mark Porter, George Wood, Cora Nix, Agnes Howard, Jewell Phillips, Gladyse Watson, Minnie Stanford, Lizzie Waldrip, Ethleen Howard, Callie Mae Watson, Nellie Lou Kellogg, Corine Collins, Dewey Mathis, Annie Grace Howard, Homer Martin, and Newman Garrett.

CUMMING ELEMENTARY FACULTY 1955 Begin Bottom Row, Left to Right

First row: Mrs. Wylene Samples, Mrs. DeEtte Bagwell, Mrs. Clara Mae Thompson, Mrs. Ellen Tallant, M Mary Sutton, Mrs. Margaret Bennett. Second row: Mrs. Euna Martin, Miss Lois White, Mrs. Ethel Nelms Miss Beulah Barron, Mrs. Betty Benson, Mrs. Dorothy Otwell, Mrs. Grace Housley, Mrs. Esther Kennemore Mrs. Marie Roper. Third row: Mrs. Verna Blackstock, Mrs. Ruth Brooks, Miss Leona Hughes, Mrs. Mary aniel, Mrs. Helen Fowler, Mrs. Edith Wright, Mrs. Frances Mize, Mrs. Frances Bearden, Mrs. Jewell Bannister, Mr. D. F. Pu am, Principal.

ARY MARTIN
Secretary

For decades, Cumming School was the center of academic, social, and cultural activities in the town. When it was constructed in 1923, it housed pupils in grades one through high school. In 1955, Forsyth County High School opened its doors, and then in 1961 Cumming Lower Elementary was established. The old Cumming School became known as Cumming Upper Elementary and served the middle grades only. When Otwell Middle School opened in the 1970s, the building was converted to administrative offices for the school system.

Eleven

Sports and
Special Happenings

Croquet was a favorite social activity around the turn of the century. It could be played by both male and female alike and required no particular strength. All that was needed was a lawn or open area, hoops, mallets, wooden balls, and stakes. A Sunday afternoon could be enjoyed in the company of friends while one played a "sport" that necessitated little exercise.

Cumming considered herself in the "big leagues" with this Cumming baseball team of 1897. Ready to take on other towns in a vigorous game were, from left to right, the following: (first row) Will Puett, Clay Bagley, Olen Merritt (mascot), Almon Hockenhull, and Marshall Groover; (second row) Arnett Hawkins, Claude Groover, and Ford Harris; (third row) Marvin Bell, Walter Otwell, and Charlie Davenport.

A birthday is a good excuse for celebration, and that is what the Kelleys did on Andy Kelley's birthday in 1898. Some of the known celebrants include the following: Virgil Martin, Kelley Pilgrim, Dr. Ansel Strickland, Roy Strickland, Hiram Kelley, Lorene Groover Vaughan, several members of the Groover and Montgomery families, John Hawkins, Jim Kelley, and Andy Kelley (fourth row, fifth adult).

The Confederate Soldiers Reunion was held in 1916 in front of the second brick courthouse on the square in Cumming. In front are members of the Cornet Band who played for the occasion. The soldier to the immediate right of the band is Forsyth County representative John L. Johnson, who was the last veteran to preside over the General Assembly of Georgia.

The Cumming Cornet Band entertained the townsfolk with Sunday afternoon concerts from the bandstand. Pictured here in 1916 were, from left to right, as follows: (front row) Leland Pirkle, Tom Kirby, Warren Brannon, Roy Otwell, Sport Merritt, Ed Kirby (director), John Ed Kirby, and Charlie Davenport; (back row) Frank Groover, Ed Merritt, Claude Hope, Oscar Hyde, Toy Otwell, and George L. Merritt.

The settlement of Cuba in the Friendship community of western Forsyth County produced a baseball team that was difficult to beat. Members of the Cuba baseball team of 1920 were, from left to right, the following: (first row) Ira Sewell (second base), Roy Redd (center field), Watt Gazaway (third base), Clyde Cox (left field), and Watt Sosebee (pitcher); (second row) Ebb Tallant (shortstop), Albert Tallant (manager), A.E. Bramblett (manager), Lint Redd (first base), and Luther Worley (catcher).

The Pirkle brothers basketball team was outstanding in the execution of the sport. The seven sons of Taylor Pirkle pictured here are, from left to right, as follows: Lewis, Frank, George, Theodore, Marshall, John, and Henry. Their father, Hebron Taylor Pirkle, a veterinarian, was born on August 28, 1882, and married Lizzie Hardin on September 1, 1905. Theodore, the oldest son, was born in 1907.

The group of Odd Fellows from Silver City Lodge posed for this picture in the 1920s. Those identified are, from left to right, as follows: (first row) unidentified, John Calvin Singleton, Thomas Hardin, George Hays, and Nelson Pirkle; (second row) unidentified, Matt Hardin, Bascomb Hughes, Jesse Norrell, Taylor Pirkle, and five unidentified; (third row) Jefferson Bennett, unidentified, Harrison Monroe, unidentified, Joshua Dooley, Andrew Bond, unidentified, and a Blanton.

Attending the Woodsmen of the Word picnic in 1924 were the following: (first row) Ezra Chadwick, two unidentified, Charlie Redd, A.W. Pruitt, George Phillips, Emory Hansard, and Doyle McWhorter; (second row) Glenn Sexton, Oscar Barnett, Dewey Gilbert, Carl Frazier, Jesse McWhorter, Curtis McWhorter, Carl McCormick, and Dewitt Fowler; (third row) Tim Moss, Loy Barnett, Kenneth Barrett, Fred Driskell, Web Martin, Wiley Mangum, Asia Odum, and Earl Frasier.

The flagpole sitter atop the Roy P. Otwell Chevrolet Agency was Watt Sosebee. He was to stay on his perch until a new 1930 Chevrolet stopped running on the sidewalk at idle speed with its wheels jacked up. If this were considered a contest, the Chevrolet won, for Sosebee came down before the idling car ran out of gasoline and stopped.

The John F. and Emily Pendley family gathered for a huge birthday celebration in 1924. Those family members identified on the second row include, from left to right, Bige Pendley, Lewis Pendley, Isaac Pendley, Jeptha Pendley, Thomas Jefferson "Bud" Pendley, Emily Adeline Martin Pendley, Martha Bennett, Susie Bennett, Virginia Bennett, Bertha Pendley Bennett, Era Pendley Martin, and Pauline Martin (baby).

For decades basketball has been a popular sport with the high school students. The Roundball Stellars from Cumming High School in 1933 were, from left to right, as follows: (first row) James Otwell, Ralph Holbrook, Joe Brooks, Henry Pirkle, and Bud Lipscomb; (second row) Coach Mack Kennemore, Garland Martin, Vernon Buice, John Harris, and "Jiggs" Bramblett.

The high school basketball teams practiced and held their games in the "Old Gym" on the second floor of the Otwell Building on Dahlonega Street. According to Gladyse Barrett, Dr. J.A. Otwell had built the two-story brick building in the 1920s. The Cumming Athletic Club and Cumming High School teams both used the gym. A small door and narrow inside steps led up to the bleachers and playing area. The fine facility lacked central heating, and the pot-bellied stove on the east side of the gym proved inadequate for supplying much warmth. Nevertheless, spectators gathered enthusiastically, and rivalry with teams from competing towns was fierce.

The need for a dam north of Atlanta was recognized in the late 1930s. After considerable political maneuvering, the U.S. Army Corps of Engineers began a feasibility study to determine the cost of constructing a dam which would facilitate navigation, flood control, and power production. On March 1, 1950, ground was broken at the site for Buford Dam, preliminary work took place, and construction followed.

Prior to construction, as seen in the photograph, land was purchased in 1953, and the first families were moved in 1954. Then a Republican administration delayed appropriations for the dam. Finally, in 1955, the Corps undertook an almost $30 million bridges and roads project in preparation for the lake which would fill behind the Buford Dam.

114

After the Corps of Engineers began filling Lake Lanier on February 1, 1956, ceremonies for the dedication of the dam were held on October 9, 1957. The keynote speaker was Georgia's Senator Richard Russell, who had striven diligently to push the Buford Dam/Lake Lanier project through the U.S. Congress. Russell favored greater action by the country in developing its water resources.

For decades Charles McCartney, better known as "Goat Man," traveled the backroads of the South with his wagon and team of goats. To support his nomadic lifestyle, he sold postcards to the scores of people who would line the highway to glimpse the unusual sight. On one such trip he was photographed as he trekked though Forsyth County. McCartney now resides in a nursing home in Macon, Georgia.

The year was 1955 and the occasion was the crowning of the "king" and "queen" at Cumming Elementary. The event culminated a fund-raiser for the school. At Halloween, the boy and girl chosen from each class would collect as much money as possible from the sale of seasonal treats. Pictured here are, from left to right, Joan Corn, Delores Wofford, Gail Bramblett, Steven Benson, David Corn, and Phil Smith.

Dancing classes with periodic recitals were held at Cumming Elementary. The dancers in this photograph are Gayle Benson, Kim Rucker, Stella Jean Carnes, Kathy McGinnis, Elaine Coots, Peggy Sudderth, Nancy Boggan, Nancy Heard, Pat Heard, Beverly Pittard, Cathy Mashburn, Linda Boling, Marguerite Mashburn, Cereta Sudderth, Mary Mashburn, Jane Wallace, Paula Heard, Diane Tinsley, Maxine Hubbard, Wanda Perry, Bill Wallace, Martha Tribble, Lera Boling, and Laura Boling.

Twelve

Business Changes

Wheeler and Wilson Sewing Machines, as the name implies, was a business suited to a pioneer economy. Few clothes were store-bought in the old days. The ladies of each household were expected to make them by hand. Farm girls were taught to card, spin, and stitch. What a joy, then, it must have been when the sewing machine came on the scene.

The Puett Hotel in its early days was called the Globe Hotel. It was also dubbed "Sawnee House." Once the home of Joseph G. Puett, the hotel stood on the east side of the courthouse square on the site of the present-day parking lot for the Forsyth Professional Building. After the building was remodeled and the lattice work removed, the once-grand old structure was turned into tenant quarters.

The first hotel in Cumming, known as the Ervin Hotel, was operated by pioneer citizen Arthur Ervin. It was located on the west side of the square near the site of Forsyth County's old log courthouse. This artistic impression of one of Cumming's earliest buildings was created by H.M. Barnes.

Dr. Hebron Taylor Pirkle (on left), a veterinarian, is pictured selling Watkins Products with dentist Dr. Maul Kelley in 1915. This self-taught and successful veterinarian was the son of Nelson Taylor Pirkle (1853–1908), who married Elizabeth Hope, daughter of Ellison and Sarah Cobb Hope, on December 28, 1876. Dr. Hebron Taylor Pirkle, born in 1882, was the couple's third child.

The Will Allen Cotton Gin was located near Brookwood Baptist Church in southern Forsyth County. The steam-powered gin was typical of other gins in the county when King Cotton was the only crop. The need for cotton gins was greatly diminished after the Depression, when cotton prices fell to all-time lows on the world market and farmers abandoned this crop for the more lucrative chicken business.

119

Alyce Redd is unpacking boxes at the back door of her father's store. She assisted her father, Ben Roper, in his general merchandise store in the Cuba settlement of the Friendship community. Later, she opened her own store, which she operated until shortly before her death, on Friendship Circle in sight of the old Roper Store building.

Benjamin P. Roper moved into the Cuba settlement in 1902 and began operating a general store beside his house. A businessman, Roper owned a cotton gin as well and served as president of the Bank of Cumming, which he also owned. In 1943, he was attacked in his store building and died a short time later. The perpetrators were apprehended, tried, and sentenced.

For a small town, Cumming has had its share of newspapers. Isaac S. Clement edited Cumming's first newspaper, the *Georgia Methodist*. The *Cumming Clarinet* began in 1875 and was later published weekly as the *Clarion*. The *Forsyth Democrat* was a short-lived paper published by William A. Porter. The *Baptist Banner* became the rival of the *Clarion*. J.S. Williams, whose slogan was "Having no fellowship with the unfaithful works of darkness," was the editor of the *Baptist Leader*. Owned by the Hightower Baptist Association, the *North Georgia Baptist*, with the slogan "Contending for the truth," appeared in 1920. The *North Georgia Baptist* underwent a name change when it was purchased by Ed Kirby. Its new name was the *North Georgian* and its slogan was "Published in the interest of religion, education, literature, and general intelligence." Kirby, two of his daughters, and three of his sons operated this enterprise.

Joe Patterson began publishing the *Forsyth County News* in 1908, and with changes in ownership and management, this paper has stood the test of time. The *Forsyth County News* remains in operation today.

121

Steam engines played a major role in the agribusiness of Forsyth County. For example, wheat threshers and mills were steam powered after the engine became widely used. It seems apropos, therefore, that Cumming's Fourth of July celebration should have evolved around the steam engine. The annual parade, started by A.G. Thomas on July 4, 1958, is still an event that draws thousands of spectators.

When Roy P. Otwell decided to go into the automobile business, he first purchased the Cumming Garage on Dahlonega Street. Later, in March 1924, he bought the Ford Agency from Roy Strickland and Louie Wisdom. Strickland and Wisdom moved to Tampa, and Roy Otwell remained entrenched in the Ford business for decades. Otwell Motors was located east of the square on Main Street.

Chickens literally saved the citizens of Forsyth County from starvation following the Great Depression and created the industry that reversed the economy of Forsyth County. When cotton failed to bring in enough revenue to sustain families of the area, the farmers began to experiment with "hot house chickens" and found that their lot in life improved substantially.

Mayor Roy Otwell's promotion of the poultry industry brought not only prosperity to the farmers but offered jobs to countless others in the processing plant in Cumming. In 1943, Otwell traveled to Chicago to convince Wilson and Company to establish a plant in Cumming. As a trial, Wilson utilized the remodeled warehouse of Roy Otwell for its first business venture in the Forsyth County area.

In addition to the old Otwell warehouse, Wilson constructed a new brick section 100 by 300 feet, which provided 40,000 square feet for the poultry processing facility. Mayor Otwell was able to direct an 8-inch main to the plant for more water and stronger pressure. When Wilson and Company's first chicken plant in Cumming proved successful for 15 years, the company purchased the adjacent land and built a modern plant, pictured here, at a cost of approximately $1 million. In the plant's early days of operation, workers processed 10,000 chickens daily. By 1980, Wilson was processing over 100,000 chickens daily and employed about 400 workers. Chickens are shipped from Cumming all over the United States and to foreign countries. Tyson's Foods has purchased the plant in recent years and has been the county's largest employer with an annual employee payroll of over $22 million.

The Forsyth County Bank was one of two modern banks on the square in Cumming. It was located on the southeast corner of the square at the intersection of Maple Street and Old Buford Road. The parking lot to the left of the present financial institution is on the site of the old Allen House, later to be the home of J.W. Fleming when he built Cumming School.

The Bank of Cumming, started by Ben Roper, was first located to the north of its later site. Roy Otwell owned the building on the northeast corner of the square, where the banking business became firmly established. Now a modern building on the northwest corner of the square at Tribble Gap Road houses the institution known until recent years as the Bank of Cumming.

The Forsyth County Hospital, established in 1957, replaced the Mary Alice Hospital, a private institution operated by the Mashburn family. Funds to construct the facility were derived from three sources—appropriations from the U.S. government made available through the Hill Burton Act and from state and local funds. This new hospital changed the methods of patient care accessible to residents of the county.

The Forsyth County Historical and Genealogical Society was organized in an attempt to assess the county's historic resources and educate the public on the history of the area. The photograph shows a booth and displays of historic documents and artifacts at a Fourth of July Parade. After operating successfully for a number of years, the society declined and was later replaced by the current historical society.

This photograph of Garland Bagley's Little Red Mill is a fitting conclusion to a volume which showcases the pictures he spent years collecting. Built by Bagley in 1975–1976 on his property at Lake Lanier, the mill is symbolic of the traditional way of life in the county. Its historic appearance and modern construction seem to appropriately link the past with the present.

Acknowledgments

With a project the magnitude of this book, the writer becomes indebted to and dependent upon the assistance of many individuals. For all who gave advice, shared knowledge, or assumed my duties to facilitate the preparation of this book, I am deeply grateful.

I wish to extend special appreciation to several persons without whose help *Forsyth County: An Album from the Garland Bagley Collection* would not have become a reality. First and foremost, to my wonderful husband, Dr. Rupert Bramblett, a native of the county, who shared his experience and knowledge of the area's past, took a special interest in the work as it progressed, exhibited patience while his wife was immersed in history, and proofread the final manuscript—I owe more than I can express. To the Historical Society of Forsyth County, especially the officers, I appreciate your support and encouragement. And for the donation of the Garland Bagley Collection to the historical society, I need to declare to Marie Roper, "You made this possible!"

Others played major roles in the project as well. Thank you to Donna Parrish, who allowed me to draw on her vast knowledge of Forsyth County and willingly discussed people and events whenever I asked for her help or advice. Thanks also to Gladyse Barrett for sharing her materials in an effort to keep Forsyth County's history alive. And to those unnamed, you are also important, for without the interest and support of Forsyth County's citizens, her heritage would be lost to future generations.